Paint

with

Words

By Anthony Swann

THE BIRCHTREE PUBLISHING GROUP, LTD.
P.O. BOX 1644
BEMIDJI, MINNESOTA 56619

Paint with Words
Copyright © 2016 by Anthony Swann

Cover and book design: Connie Knutson
Cover design copyright © 2016 Birchtree Publishing Group Ltd.
Editor: Joanna Dymond

ISBN 978-0-692-03274-9

Printed in the United States of America

Introduction by Carol Ann Russell, Ph.D.

I first encountered the poet-jazz-man, Anthony Swann, when he stepped inside the Cosmic Java Coffee House in Bemidji, Minnesota one autumn night on Beltrami Avenue. It was raining, and Anthony rode a bike, and if I remember right, we invited both to shelter within! I was there as the advisor to a B.S.U. student writer group, Rivers Meeting Project, newly founded in 1991 to celebrate poetry. Clearly this was Anthony's family (or "his People") –a group of renegade writers who took their love of words and writing outside the walls of "academe," on to the sidewalks of Bemidji, "our little town." The Java had a small raised corner stage for reading and playing music that was open to all. Anthony liked the scene, and returned nearly every week on Wednesday nights, to join us and we claimed him for our own. That was nearly twenty-five years ago.

In your hands, you are holding a print volume of Anthony's poetry, a treasure of language. Although Anthony is well known for his reading aloud poems, this volume upholds the work's true literary merit. I believe it is an indivisible love-- of words, song, art, and jazz-- which makes Anthony Swann unique as poet. In Anthony's imagination, everything belongs! The canons of art and literature give way to a tribal vision, a rainbow bridge to the "dream-time" of our common American Soul. For in history and at heart, we Americans are all drifters and mixed-bloods, and none of us really "belong" to the blue bloodlines of European art. Thus, Anthony writes for U.S.

Anthony Swann has claimed Effie, Minnesota as the Omphalos of the little Midwest, our common home. Yet it takes a real poet, a poet with an ear to make us whole: *"These are my people. . . all focused on The Sound, The Holy Sound. . .a long lost train thru America that's coming home."* The reality is, Anthony Swann is a rebel outside and inside of time. His wanderings across America have not just been highways but the ley lines, and his ear is a human ear, his heart our beating heart: *"I keep salsa going in my head that I may live in the company of poets while Wonder turns their worlds round like the worlds of children making song my province."*

Anthony is a life-long member of another group of song and poem makers, those recognized and welcomed by the esteemed Black American poet, Etheridge Knight, who began the legendary gatherings in bars and diners and run-down cafes which he called Free Peoples. Whenever I taught a rogue course at the university, from "The Tao of Poetry" to "Rebel Voices," Anthony was there. Inevitably, and because Anthony Swann was among us, in the same room, these younger writers felt more free! He would come in just as class was beginning, sit quietly in the back, until we re-formed the group into a circle of real people. Then, without fanfare, Anthony would join in, bringing music to share, poems to read aloud, videotapes of old writers, and books long out of print which he shared with anyone who would borrow. In his quiet and brilliant way, Anthony would shine. Who else would dare pair Beethoven with "Magic Carpet Ride" Steppenwolf? Yet another toast to his inspired "family" through time! All are but the archetypal "old men dancing" with the Shell Goddess in Las Vegas between Tropicana Avenue and the clock-less casino. Here are poems of spiritual and cultural witness to the "blindness" of capitalism vanquished by the "vision" of all Fools for Love—and these be We Free Poets indeed.

Carol Ann Russell
Poet & Professor
M.F.A.; Ph.D.

*Author of four collections of poetry, two chapbooks, and a letter-press edition in English and Italian: **The Red Envelope; Feast; Silver Dollar; Gypsy Taxi; Without Reservation; Lost on Highway 61-Streaming Live; and PASSEGIATTA.** Professor of English and Creative Writing at Bemidji State University since 1988, Carol Ann Russell has been recognized for her poetry by regional, national, and international publications and awards.*

Table of Contents

Pissarro heading outside to paint, pushing a special easel built to roll through the fields.

Paint with Words

Squeeze them out of their tubular cases
to send them romping across canvas.
Toss and smear them into messy melanges.
Encourage their fornication and oily orgies
to create babies of the new *avant garde*.
Spread them thickly with big flat brushes into Russian novels
or tickle them with fine pointed brushes into delicate poems.

Spread-eagle plot on canvas.
Nail it down! Make it do your bidding.
Drive out exposition like Christ drove out the moneylenders
so your characters speak for themselves.
Like Pissarro put wheels on his easel,
take up your notebook and go *plein air*.
Take color from sky, flower, sun.

Climb upward to the goats and windmills of Montmartre
where poets and painters speak for each other
wording with paint,
painting with words.

Saint Lucia
Virign Martyr
Patron of the Blind and Protector of Eyesight

Saint Lucia of Syracuse

Lucia,

Saint of Syracuse, Sicily,

You wore a wreath of candles

lighting tunnels to bring food to

persecuted Christians.

Van Gogh, too wore a hat with

candles atop, his for painting at night.

He too worked with the poor.

When Roman soldiers gouged out

your eyes, Lucia, you could still see. In

icon you hold your eyeballs

on a tray. Van Gogh offers his ear. Light still pours into the world

from you both, shines from Vincent's paintings in great galleries

and from the wreaths of candles girls wear on your feast day

to light up our dark winters.

Lady of Light,

please protect the eyesight of our artist friends

for whom the world is a visual feast.

Come to us, O Holy Saint, with your halo of light

that we may see within

light we share deep in our souls.

The Mighty Wrens of Chicago

Amid the cavernous city's clamor,

roar of huge trucks, busses, trains,

lines of cars like hungry millipedes,

the human multitudes expressing themselves,

oration of dignitaries,

exclamations of tourists, celebrity appearances,

workers, shouts and cries of the captains, the muscled men

 who lift up skyscrapers, run stockyards and docks,

the famous jazz of the city, the blues in the basements,

amid all the din and symphony

there's YOU, tiny Wrens,

least of these,

humbler than the ever present pigeons, specks of spirit,

little brown pieces of God hopping about sidewalks and busy

streets stirring my heart more than the great lions guarding The

Art Institute, making me smile at your verve,

your insistence, Citizen Wrens,

Chicago is yours.

I Celebrate the Common Dandelion

"Man has yet to learn to live with the weeds."
~ Ohshinnah Fast Wolf

I celebrate the common dandelion,

burgeoning, bold, suddenly springing Spring-song,

yellow exclamation punctuating green,

fecundly abundant in riotous profusion,

joyful as the golden sun and children

for whom there are no "weeds",

friendly to bees and wine-makers,

reliable-integral-essential,

valient in gloried warrior days,

undaunted by human hatred and pesticides,

raising victory-banner seed globes perfectly round, dissolving into

wind, seed-scattered like new nations. What a shame for perfect

lawn people:

A common "weed" victor over man!

The Shell Goddess

Waves, hands of the Goddess caressing beaches,
leave necklaces of shells to adorn them.
That Goddess who guides the trail of smallest snail,
fashioned the giant conch,
chambered the pearly nautilus
and set her signature, the spiral, in the shells,
salutations to her.

Her subtle yin/yang energies form spirals
like twisting winds tornados or water swirls,
her signatures spiral-spun throuhout creation
     in the double-helix of DNA,
       the whorl of hair at the backs of our heads,
       in our spiral-shaped ears.

That Goddess of serpent-power lying Kundalini-coiled
in subtle body chakra who spins our lives on her secret
spindles, that Goddess is the authoress
 of how we move in circles tightening round
truth to realize its liberation, circling
love until it teaches us to sing.

The Buffalo

The buffalo

is the shape the plains take

when they move.

Autumn

The f_alling

dr_ifti ng

leaves

say more than a hundred politicians.

Wintergreen

Look! Wintergreen

Imagine green leaves and blood-red jewels

peeking through snow!

Grandma Calling

1. Feral Feeding

Today, in honor of Grandma,
I fed a group of wild city cats
spooning out three large cans of cat food
to divide on two large platters.
They swarmed, head to head,
ignoring me until the food was gone
then backed away, finding cover.

Every afternoon Grandma would step outside and yell
"Here kitty kitty kitty KIT-EEEEEEEEEEEEEEEEEEEE!"
Cats came from everywhere, house and woods,
everywhere in between,
wild and tame, young and old, fat and skinny,
spotted, striped, cats of all colors, combinations
thereof and dispositions.
She fed them all scraps of meat or fish and whole milk.
That is the standard.

As a farm girl in South Carolina
she knew the muzzle-warmth of critters,
talked to them and they to her,
became animal talker,
without raising a hand could call off
the waddling neck-protruding geese
who, to protect their young,
bit anyone who tried to reach the house.
The bond of trust and love between Grandma
and the animals was a strong language of its own.

2. The Call

Hark sister! Grandma's calling from the other world!
coming through dream to wood's edge
beckoning us to cross the yard to where
the giant white pine spreads its roots
and feral cats slip into the forest.

"Don't let them tame you," she whispers.
"Mother Nature soothes but she's also warrior,
turns revolutions in soil, appears in flocks of vulture.
People will sell out the land, poison rivers.
Don't be docile."

"Remember when the lynx came to my yard's edge
to peer into the perimeter of civilization,
its green eyes aglow with eerie supernatural light,
that lynx, sacredly wild beyond- compromise,
shall forever be more vital than tame cats.
Don't let them tame you."

I call out to Grandma in the dream:
"0 Gramma, you died before Sister and I
could tell you how much we love you!"
Grandma takes the curlers out of her hair,
puts in her false teeth, smiles,
says: "Be kind to children and critters."

Effie, Minnesota is the Center of the Universe

When crossing northern Minnesota or coming up on the scenic drive from Grand Rapids from Northhome to Ely

There's a feeling I get when I come upon the open-fielded crossroads called Effie, apart from the usual crossroads store, cafe and bar, the area all around feels like an open stage where wilderness gives way to important things about to happen. things broad, grand and swinging like big band jazz or subtle as secret epiphanies.

Effie has rodeos and beer tasting events but I also expect something beyond the scope of Chamber of Commerce, more cosmic. It's in the air, intangible yet certain, as if you stopped for a moment at the center of the universe, poised at a cosmic pivot as important as say New York or a Himalayan Ashram. For what is New York but a puzzle of streets, corner stores and precincts and ashram but a hall full of huddled aspirants.

Effie is oasis. A traveler draws water and rest and the spirit dances with a joy as open as its four directions.

These Are My People

These are my people
the jazz babies
the hangers on
second liners
the thrill kids
on or off the sauce
who hang around the funk-pit clubs at night,
saxophones soaring like hawks
a Slo-Gin slow blues pouring out the door
into nights of carnal film-noire pleasure
and backed-up cold turkey pain,
on their runs or comin' off
moving like animated panthers,
loose-jointed Mick Jaggers,
Symphony Sids on the prowl,
looking for kicks
but mostly the good deep pleasure
in The Sound, The Holy Sound, man,

that came outa The Big Easy, Chi-Town, St. Louis, Memphis,

52nd St., and K.C., man, and moved into the

heart of a country, too white and full of hate,

to see a good thing, on bargain basement vinyl

and Duke Ellington went unrecognized until

his sophistication just overcame it all,

and The Count came over the radio

and later Miles and Mingus prowled stages like shamans

all focused on The Sound, The Holy Sound.

These are my people

coming to hear the music and have a beer

to cram loins in lusty dance

or just relax, rap, share and signify.

Yes, these are my people

and the blues in the night,

a long lost train thru America that's coming home,

that's my music.

Blue Trailings

(Parker's Road Song)
For Charlie "Bird" Parker

Unlikely to join anybody's fraternity,
making others see themselves,
moving among you freely like a great railway porter's ghost,
gigging, dancing, I'm blowing.

On a mountain slope a puma grins,
osprey circles above, fish cradled in talon,
lizard's belly scrapes rock.
When hobo leaves his ditchside bed,
comes down the deserted road in twilight, I'll be blowing;
I was blowing when he laid his head in the tall ditch grass
all wet with dew.
When the train rides lone in the desert,
sunlighted like a silver snake shinning,
I am blowing.
I was blowing when, circling high, the hawk
first caught the glint of the train's twisting silver.

In those moments wherein the inspiration and execution are one;
in the eternal song, I am blowing, in the song unsung.
I was blowing upon the altar, phoenix-bound,
in the ash and eden simultaneously.

All the roads I have run,

my fingers race sax keys flawlessly,

a song I cannot end, song without beginning,

I am blowing, blowing,

Coming in for a real roost,

Coming home to where they jump the blues.

JUMP UP KANSAS CITY! HOME FREE!

I Keep Salsa Going In My Head

For Pete Velezquez and The Mission District,
San Francisco, 1964.

I keep salsa going in my head

trumpets and congas

groovy latin piano

funky sharp rhythm,

slow, earthy like quajira, or rapido

like pachanga, rhumba, mambo or cha cha cha.

I love the way latinos move around

the dance floor, long to plunge

into a sea of latin dancers,

dark sea, in which Motion has

found her proper field of play,

beauty in liquid forms flowing,

flashing laughter, pride, beauty and grace.

Continuous rhythm, ever running like a friend for life
rolling from bandstands, living in the hearts and bodies of the
bloods like the soft wary motion of the spirit of life.

I hear congas laying a foundation beat solid as African earth,
the bassist building a frame for a house of song,
timbales spitting out rhythm orgies
while flutes and trumpets dance above
teasing melody which the pianist flourishes.

I keep salsa going in my head
that I may live in the company of poets
while Wonder turns their worlds round
like the worlds of children
making song my province.
You will find me
right at the heart of the rhythm.

Blind Lemon Jefferson's Last Gig

December, 1929
Blind Lemon Jefferson was found frozen in the snow
after playing blues at a Chicago house party.
We can't know what went on
that cold winter night in the Windy City.
No historian can recreate those real people,
a movie never made.
All we know is there was need
for a musician to play feel good music,
blues medicine for red blooded people.
Blood was pulsing,
beer flowed, whiskey poured, dance cut loose.
In the sweat/funk there was pleasure/release.

All we know is Blind Lemon Jefferson needed to do
what was most essential, play blues, needed the pay.
We don't know how much he suffered as he lay freezing
in the snow, we don't know, don't know.
All we know is musicians, sane or crazy,
play for us all our lives
and more than anything else
keep us keeping on.

Song Sparks

If skylarks sing jazz riffs that storm the gates of heaven
and male humpback whales improvise songs for their females
then angels must sing arias and God Herself be song,
continuous cosmic love song,
notes emanating to become worlds, reaching out,
becoming living beings filled with song sparks.

Even cocky rogues like Jelly Roll Morton and Sidney Bechet
must've had God's glow about them as they did
the brothel strut, bragging of sexual conquest, the invention of jazz.
Maybe that joy we catch from song
is reflection varying vibes
of heavenly jam session
the universe singing in the key of OM
declaring song is home
while in air bees buzz, birds hum
and in earth, a music of mushrooms and moles.

Columba

There is in our love the quality of adoration.

Bearing gifts we meet at the altar

for the Greater Gift, our caresses worship.

A mystic union with eternal hope.

And fled with the phoenix's flash,

the sacrifice without wounds,

awaiting always the Greater Glory.

White-winged have you touched me, O Dove,

white-winged, hope-hastening, dream-derived,

eternity's ebb pinion-poised

as sea-sounding some solar small shell.

Symbol-stricken, mutually-muted,

no earthly symbol have I,

save that my happiness is white in color,

unutterable in voice, unfettered in realm,

light with the weight of eternity.

O little bird of great embracing wingspan!

Tea Time

Having discarded old bones of calcium, the spirit sallies forth

through the planes to await further incarnation and

smiling Japanese Zen masters serenely sip green tea

while eternity breaks evenly like a huge wave

rippling boa-constrictor fashion throughout the universe.

Mr. Planter's Peanut, with his cane, and Snoopy

are featured on giant billboards across the moon

proclaiming love and cosmic indigestion.

Mister Fantasy steps out of Golden Gate Park, having finished a gig

on Hippie Hill with the spade conga drummers and

all the computers extant and to be

enter a vortex of vanishment at the center of the Pentagon.

Beethoven Mad in the Streets

Beethoven mad in the streets

cursing mumbling to himself like Steppenwolf

hung-over and freshly drunk on wine

stumbling on litter

food particles on his expensive but smelly week-old clothes hair unkempt

people stare at Beethoven

peg him as alcoholic stumblebum

he shouts at them or ignores them

walks on aimlessly

his hoary head buzzin' full of melodies immortal

ideas he turns into masterpieces

later falling womanless into an unkempt bed,

angels watching over him as he snores.

BEETHOVEN OUT WALKING (c. 1820)
Pencil drawing by Josef Daniel Böhm (1794–1865)
Beethoven-Haus, Bonn, H. C. Bodmer Collection

Las Vegas Native

We walked parallel, roadrunner and I,
he along a golf-course fence,
I toward work down Tropicana Avenue
He looked amused as he watched me
while I admired the exact rhythm
of his power-charged steps,
a tuft of feathers at his crown
which rose then subsided
at exactly the same number of steps.

I suddenly realized roadrunner belonged,
rooted like the Paiute in the Mojave,
his ancestors power-striding the meadow water-hole
 to strike little lizards
long before the Spaniards,Mormons and train-stop
while I, a transplant,
lived and worked in a mirage of money/concrete
and transported palms white men poured
into the valley basin filling it mountain to mountain
with tracts and clock-less casino.

Old Men Dancing

Yuppies think they're hip now ordering expensive rum drinks
with mint or lime mashed with a wooden stick.
Hell, in Brazil caipirinha is the national drink. Cachaca, cheap
cane rum, straight will knock you on your ass. They mash limes at
home, add sugar and cachaca to fuel their partied nights, samba
and soccer.
I drank it in my little pension room listening to the drunks howl
song like coyotes in the courtyard of the bar below,
drank the same essence of Brazil in a bottle black slaves drank
in the 1500's who were brought in to work the sugar mills.
I drank it in a little neighborhood stand-up bar before a
Brazilian wedding, drank it alone again watching one of
those enormous juicy tropical cockroaches crawl to the top
of my bottle seeking sweet, drank it til I saw skeletons
dance in my brain. I drank it at a samba band rehearsal
and danced with an old black man from Bahia, his wife long
dead, me without a girl, we just danced together.

At a dance once I saw an old man drunk on wine and dancing
alone out dance all the fancy dancers.
Now I'm an old man dancing through a sober life alone.
Soon I'll be tottering with a staff but I know in my soul
I'm still the fire in the finest Latin drummers, the power
of endurance in the oldest pines.

I may have been a falling-down-piss-on-myself drunk

but I know the secret:

Jesus wasn't jivin' when He said show me the stone

which the builder has rejected.

I will make it the cornerstone.

The Brazilian beggars I saw on the steps

of the cathedral, the street kids in Rio the goons shoot

and dump, the AIDS victims, the lepers of the world

and all us drunks, reformed or not,

are the source I long for

in a sea of spirit shining

filled with the fire of God.

The Fool To The King

Fool: If thou wert my fool, nuncle, I'd have thee
          beaten for being old before thy time.
Lear: How's that?
Fool: Thou shoudst not have been old till thou
          hadst been wise.

                ~ Shakespeare, King Lear, Act 1, Scene 5.

What, King?

Hast thou forgotten, in thy greed, how to laugh, to love,

to make music?

It is my job to humor, thee yet how can I proceed in jest

when thou hast cast evil all about us?

Thou dost choke on thy own gristle

and undigested events the wind blows back on thee.

Think thou canst play foul chess with weaker nations, plucking

them about, killing kings, replacing them with lackey surrogates?

Dropping a burning-oil-death from the sky like evil rain?

Thou art left howling like Lear in a storm of thine own making,

split like a skunk tween pride of its odor yet sick in it.

Once smug, secure, how you do now unravel

and haunt the broken house of capitalism!

      Who indeed can the fool now be

      When you have alienated all but me?

The Great Purification
(After the Hopi)

"We danced, O Brave, we danced beyond their farms.
In cobalt desert closures made our vows ....
Now is the strong prayer folded in thine arms, The serpent
with the eagle in the boughs."

From "The Bridge: The Dance"
by Hart Crane

Before the machines and anti-organic world,

remember to what heights we dreamed

and soared for the infinite

when the whole world was a living entity

to our people, even the rocks sang ...

Remember how we watched the tender green spiral

at the center of our beautiful corn plants

rise upward to bear the flesh we would be remade of ...

Remember when, under blue mesa sky,

in thin, cool air,

our priests communed with the Spirits ...

Through ages we kept vigil with prayer and ceremony

but now too many others take a forked path

chosing destructive technology over our Earth Mother,

turning backs to Her.

Now it is time for The Great Purification.